www.booksbyboxer.com

No part of this publication may be reproduced or transmitted in any form or by any means, electronic or mechanical, including photocopying, recording or any information storage and retrieval system, or for the source of ideas without written permission from the publisher.

Bee Three Publishing is an imprint of Books By Boxer
Published by
Books By Boxer, Leeds, LS13 4BS, UK
Books by Boxer (EU), Dublin, D02 P593, IRELAND
Boxer Gifts LLC, 955 Sawtooth Oak Cir, VA 22802, USA
© Books By Boxer 2024
All Rights Reserved
MADE IN CHINA
ISBN: 9781915410771

This book is produced from responsibly sourced paper to ensure forest management

THE ART OF COFFEE VOCAB:

ACIDITY:
The bright, tangy, or crisp quality of coffee, often described as lively or sparkling.

AROMA:
The fragrance of brewed coffee, influenced by the beans' origin, roast, and brewing method.

BODY:
The mouthfeel or weight of the coffee on the palate, ranging from light to full.

BLOOM:
The initial release of gases (mainly carbon dioxide) from coffee grounds when hot water is first poured over them.

CREMA:
The golden, creamy layer that forms on top of a well-extracted espresso shot.

EXTRACTION:
The process of dissolving coffee flavors from the grounds into water during brewing.

GRIND SIZE:
The size of the coffee particles after grinding, which affects extraction and flavor.

LATTE ART:
Designs created on the surface of espresso drinks using steamed milk.

PORTAFILTER:
The handle and filter basket assembly used in an espresso machine to hold the coffee grounds.

ROAST:
The process of heating coffee beans to develop flavor; can be light, medium, or dark.

SINGLE-ORIGIN:
Coffee sourced from one location, farm, or region, highlighting its unique characteristics.

TAMPING:
Pressing down coffee grounds in the portafilter to ensure even extraction during brewing.

ESPRESSO:
A concentrated coffee brewed by forcing hot water through finely-ground coffee under high pressure.

UNRAVELING THE ORIGINS OF 'COFFEE'!

The captivating tale of 'coffee' commences with the Arabic word 'Quawah,' where it was initially hailed as the 'wine of the bean'.

This rich brew, with its tantalizing aroma and invigorating taste, quickly captured the hearts of those who savored it.

As its popularity spread, so did its name, taking on new forms as it traversed regions and cultures.

The Ottoman Turks played a significant role in shaping the linguistic landscape of coffee, affectionately referring to it as 'Kahve.'

Under the Ottoman Empire's reign, coffeehouses flourished, becoming vibrant hubs of social interaction.

The Dutch, renowned for their exploration and trade ventures, left a mark on the global spread of coffee. Transforming the Ottoman 'Kahve' into 'Koffie,' they introduced the beverage to new corners of the world, fueling its rise to prominence.

However, the most intriguing linguistic twist occurred in 1582, when the English word 'Coffee' made its debut.

This marked a crucial moment in the beverage's evolution, as it transcended linguistic barriers and became firmly rooted in the English lexicon.

From the exotic 'Quawah' to the familiar 'Coffee,' this caffeinated elixir has traversed continents, changing names but never losing its allure. Its journey reflects the interconnectedness of cultures and the enduring fascination with this cherished beverage.

So, raise your cup to the rich tapestry of history woven into every sip of coffee, reminding us of the timeless allure of exploration and discovery.

BEAN ETIQUETTE:

Tip #1

Choose beans from a reputable roaster, not the bargain bin at the grocery store. Think of it like dating – you want quality, not just what's convenient.

Store your beans in an airtight container, away from light, heat, and nosy roommates.

Avoid the fridge; coffee beans hate the cold as much as you do on a Monday morning.

Use a digital kitchen scale. Eyeballing it is for spaghetti, not coffee.

Start with a 1:15 ratio (1 gram of coffee to 15 grams of water). Adjust to taste, because coffee is personal, like your Spotify playlist.

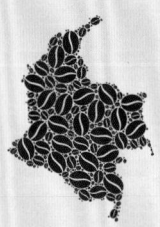

A COLOMBIAN COLLABORATION!

On June 15th, 2019, in the coffee-loving nation of Colombia, a remarkable event took place. A team of fifty dedicated individuals came together with one mission: to brew the largest cup of coffee the world had ever seen.

This monumental endeavor wasn't just about making a massive pot of joe; it was a celebration of Colombia's rich coffee culture and a testament to the nation's love for the beloved beverage.

The result? A staggering 22,739.14 liters of freshly brewed coffee – enough to fill a small swimming pool! This colossal cup of java wasn't just for show; it was a genuine Guinness World Record-breaking achievement, recognized and celebrated around the globe.

Imagine the aroma wafting through the air as this mammoth cup of coffee was brewed – it must have been an unforgettable experience for everyone involved.

And while the sheer volume of coffee brewed that day is impressive enough, what's even more remarkable is the teamwork and coordination required to pull off such a feat.

From sourcing the beans to brewing the brew, every step of the process required meticulous planning and execution.

But for the people of Colombia, it was all worth it – after all, what better way to showcase their passion for coffee than by creating a world record-breaking cup of the finest Colombian java?

So the next time you sip on your morning cup of coffee, take a moment to appreciate the incredible effort and dedication that went into brewing the world's largest cup of coffee in Colombia.

POUR OVER

EQUIPMENT NEEDED:
· Pour-over dripper · Coffee filter (paper or cloth) ·
Freshly ground coffee beans · Kettle
· Timer · Mug or carafe

STEP 1
Heat water to about 200°F (93°C). If you don't have a thermometer, bring the water to a boil and let it sit for about 30 seconds.

STEP 2
Place the filter in the dripper and rinse it with hot water. This removes any paper taste and preheats the dripper. Discard the rinse water.

STEP 3
For a standard 12-ounce cup, use about 20 grams of coffee and 300 grams of water.

STEP 4
Place the dripper on top of your mug or carafe. Add the ground coffee to the filter and gently shake to level the grounds. Start your timer and pour enough water to wet all the grounds evenly. Let it sit for about 30-45 seconds.

STEP 5
After the bloom, continue pouring water slowly in a circular motion, starting from the center and moving outward, then back to the center. Continue pouring until you reach your desired water weight. The total brewing time should be around 3-4 minutes.

STEP 6
Once the water has passed through the grounds, remove the dripper and discard the filter and spent grounds. Give your coffee a gentle swirl to mix and serve immediately.

UNLEASH THE FLAVOR POWER!

Tip #2

Use filtered water, not the stuff that tastes like your swimming pool.

Filtered water removes impurities and chemicals like chlorine, which can affect the taste of your coffee.

Using filtered water ensures consistency in flavor from one brew to the next, so your morning cup is always just right.

Filtered water also helps prevent scale buildup, keeping your equipment in top shape for longer.

BEETHOVEN'S MUSICAL MUSE: COFFEE!

Ludwig van Beethoven, the iconic composer whose music has inspired millions, had a lesser-known passion: coffee.

Yes, the man who gave us timeless symphonies and sonatas was also a devoted coffee enthusiast. Beethoven's love for coffee was so intense that he had a very specific routine for brewing his favorite drink.

Beethoven's method was nothing short of meticulous. He insisted on precisely 60 coffee beans per cup – no more, no less. Legend has it that he would count each bean himself, ensuring that his morning brew was perfect every time.

This attention to detail might seem a bit eccentric, but for Beethoven, it was just another expression of his artistic temperament.

Coffee was more than just a beverage for Beethoven; it was a daily ritual that fueled his creativity.

He would often start his day with a strong cup of coffee, finding inspiration and energy in its rich, aromatic embrace.

In a way, coffee was the unseen companion in the creation of some of his greatest works, from the dramatic "Symphony No. 5" to the sublime "Für Elise".

Beethoven's dedication to his coffee routine reflects the composer's broader approach to life and art.

Just as he strove for perfection in his music, he sought the same level of excellence in his daily coffee. It's a delightful reminder that even the greatest geniuses have their simple pleasures and routines that keep them grounded.

COFFEE
IS A HUG
IN A MUG

BREWING BRILLIANCE WITH TEMPERATURE!

Tip #3

Boil the water and then let it sit for about 30 seconds to 1 minute to cool slightly. This generally brings the temperature down to the desired range.

Water that is too cool (below 195°F) will under-extract the coffee, resulting in weak, sour, and underwhelming flavors.

Water that is too hot (above 205°F) can over-extract the coffee, leading to bitter and harsh flavors.

The optimal water temperature for brewing coffee is between 195°F and 205°F.

For the most accuracy, use a thermometer to measure the water temperature.

TYPES OF ROASTS

LIGHT ROASTS

Light brown colored.
No oil seen on surface.
Fruity and acidic flavor.

MEDIUM ROASTS

Medium brown colored.
Flavor, acidity, and aroma
are sweet and balanced.

MEDIUM - DARK ROASTS

Dark brown colored.
Some oil on surface.
Flavor and aroma is stronger.
Bittersweet aftertaste.

DARK ROASTS

Black colored.
Oily surface.
Bitter and rich flavor
and aroma.

FRENCH PRESS

EQUIPMENT NEEDED:
· French press · Freshly ground coffee beans ·
Kettle · Timer · Stirring utensil

STEP 1
water to about 200°F (93°C). If you don't have a thermometer, bring the water to a boil and let it sit for about 30 seconds.

STEP 2
standard 34-ounce (1 liter) French press, use about 56 grams of coffee. Grind the coffee to a coarse consistency, similar to breadcrumbs.

STEP 3
Pour a small amount of hot water into the French press to preheat it, then discard the water.

STEP 4
d the coarsely ground coffee to the French press. Start your timer and pour hot water over the coffee grounds. r slowly and evenly to ensure all the grounds are saturated. Use about half of the total water initially.

STEP 5
about 30 seconds, stir the grounds gently to break the crust and ensure even extraction. Add the remaining water to the French press.

STEP 6
Place the lid on the French press with the plunger pulled all the way up. Let the coffee steep for 4 minutes.

STEP 7
er 4 minutes, slowly and steadily press the plunger down to arate the grounds from the brewed coffee. Pour the coffee immediately into your mug or a carafe. Enjoy!

CHEW BEFORE BREW: THE COFFEE CHRONICLES!

Long before coffee met hot water, there was the original coffee chew!

Ancient African tribes would grind coffee berries, toss in some animal fat, and craft chewable balls of caffeinated awesomeness.

Yep, coffee used to be a portable, energy-boosting snack – it was basically the world's first caffeine gum!

While today we sip, back then, they nibbled their way to a java jolt. Coffee history: where every chew was a coffee adventure!

DON'T CRY OVER SPOILED BEANS!

Tip #4

Use an airtight container to protect the beans from exposure to air, which can cause oxidation and stale flavors. Ceramic or stainless steel containers are ideal.

Light, especially sunlight, can degrade coffee beans. Store your coffee in a dark, opaque container to block out light.

Coffee beans should be kept dry. Moisture can lead to mold growth and spoil the beans.

Whole beans stay fresh longer than pre-ground coffee.

If you buy a large amount of coffee, consider dividing it into smaller portions and storing them in separate airtight containers.

BRAZIL'S COFFEE JOURNEY TO THE OLYMPICS!

In 1932, Brazil had Olympic dreams that were as big and bold as a freshly brewed cup of coffee. However, the country faced a significant hurdle: financial constraints threatened to keep its athletes from participating in the Los Angeles Summer Olympics.

The Brazilian government found itself in a tight spot, struggling to gather enough funds to send their sports heroes across the globe.

But in a country where coffee is more than just a drink – it's a cultural icon and economic powerhouse – a creative solution was brewing.

Brazil decided to turn to its beloved coffee beans to fund the Olympic dream.

These beans weren't just along for the ride; they were the ticket to California, each one representing a small piece of Brazilian ambition and determination.

In a bold and unprecedented move, the government loaded the athletes and a ship full of coffee beans onto a vessel named "Itaquicê". As the ship set sail across the Atlantic, those coffee beans became tiny ambassadors of Brazilian perseverance and ingenuity.

The plan was simple yet brilliant: sell the coffee in ports along the journey to raise the necessary funds for the athletes to reach Los Angeles.

By the time the ship reached the shores of California, the proceeds from this java-fueled adventure had added up to the necessary funds. Brazil's athletes, fueled by the power of coffee and the support of their nation, were ready to compete on the world stage.

This coffee-powered journey to the Olympics proves that when your dreams are grand, even the humblest of beans can kickstart the sweetest victories.

TODAY'S GOOD MOOD

PROUDLY SPONSORED BY COFFEE

AEROPRESS

EQUIPMENT NEEDED:
· AeroPress · AeroPress filter ·
Freshly ground coffee beans · Kettle
· Stirring utensil · Timer · Mug or carafe

STEP 1
Heat water to about 175°F to 185°F (80°C to 85°C) for a less bitter coffee, or up to 200°F (93°C) for a stronger brew.

STEP 2
Place a paper filter in the AeroPress cap and rinse it with water to remove any paper taste and preheat the equipment. Discard the rinse water.

STEP 3
For a standard AeroPress, use about 14-18 grams of coffee. d the coffee to a medium-fine consistency, similar to table salt.

STEP 4
e the AeroPress on top of your mug or carafe with the filter cap rewed on. Add the ground coffee to the AeroPress chamber.

STEP 5
art your timer and pour hot water over the coffee grounds up he desired level. Stir the coffee slurry for about 10-15 seconds to ensure even saturation.

STEP 6
t the plunger into the chamber to create a seal, but do not press et. Let the coffee steep for about 1-2 minutes. After the steeping ne, press the plunger down slowly and steadily until you hear a hissing sound, indicating all the water has passed through the coffee grounds.

STEP 7
Dilute with hot water if desired, or enjoy the coffee as a concentrated shot.

COFFEE CREATES FIZZ!

When you choose decaf coffee, you're part of a fascinating process that goes beyond your morning brew.

Coffee beans undergo a unique transformation to shed their caffeine. This process involves various methods like water processing, carbon dioxide extraction, or using chemical solvents to remove the caffeine content from the beans while preserving their flavor.

But what happens to the extracted caffeine? It doesn't go to waste! Instead, it finds a second life in the soda and pharmaceutical sectors.

This recycled caffeine becomes a key ingredient in a variety of products, including soft drinks, energy drinks, and over-the-counter medications like pain relievers and cold remedies.

So, when we choose decaf, we're not just making a coffee choice; we're indirectly contributing to the caffeine supply for soda and pharmaceuticals.

This additional source of caffeine helps boost the production of these products, ensuring they meet the high demand for caffeinated beverages and effective medications.

It's a surprising ripple effect from your daily coffee selection!

By opting for decaf, you're playing a part in a larger supply chain that keeps the wheels of other industries turning.

This interconnectedness highlights the intricate ways in which our everyday choices can impact a wide range of products and sectors, in this case, all stemming from the humble coffee bean.

DON'T LET COFFEE BE A GRIND!

Tip #5

Grinding your coffee beans just before brewing ensures a fresh, flavorful cup. Use a burr grinder for consistent grind size, which is crucial for optimal extraction.

Different brewing methods require specific grind sizes:

- **Coarse for French press**
- **Medium-coarse for pour-over**
- **Medium for drip coffee**
- **Medium-fine for AeroPress**
- **Fine for espresso**
- **Extra-fine for Turkish coffee**

Grind only the amount needed before brewing to preserve freshness.

Measure beans with a scale for accuracy, clean your grinder regularly to avoid flavor contamination, and adjust grind size to taste—coarser for less bitterness, finer for less sourness. Consistency is key for even extraction and better flavor.

MY Blood type IS Coffee

WORLD'S OLDEST COFFEE-LOVING CAT

The oldest cat in recorded history, named Crème Puff, holds the Guinness World Record for her remarkable longevity.

Crème Puff lived an astonishing 38 years, from August 3, 1967, to August 6, 2005.

Her daily routine included an unusual treat for a feline: a sip of coffee every day. But her unique diet didn't stop there.

Crème Puff's owner, Jake Perry, fed her a daily diet consisting of bacon, broccoli, and eggs, a combination not typically associated with feline cuisine.

This unconventional diet seemed to work wonders, contributing to her record-breaking lifespan.

Interestingly, Crème Puff's predecessor, Grandpa Rex Allen, also enjoyed a long life of 34 years under Perry's care.

Grandpa Rex Allen, the previous record holder, followed the same diet of bacon, broccoli, and eggs, along with daily coffee.

Given the consistent results with both cats, it raises intriguing questions about the impact of diet and care on feline longevity.

Jake Perry's approach to cat care, combining an unusual diet with attentive, loving care, seems to defy conventional wisdom.

While it's not scientifically proven that this specific diet led to such impressive lifespans, the consistent results with two of the oldest cats in recorded history suggest that Perry's methods might have played a significant role. Coincidence? We think not!

COFFEEHOUSE DEBUT: BREWING IN 1555!

In 1555, coffeehouses emerged as vibrant social hubs, marking a pivotal moment in the history of coffee culture.

The first coffeehouse in the world was established in Istanbul, then part of the Ottoman Empire.

Coffee, which had been gaining popularity in Arabian countries for its stimulating properties and social appeal, found a new home in these bustling establishments.

Coffeehouses quickly became more than just places to drink coffee; they were centers of social activity, intellectual discourse, and cultural exchange.

People from all walks of life gathered in these establishments to engage in lively discussions, conduct business negotiations, play games like chess or backgammon, and even recite poetry.

However, not everyone embraced the rise of coffeehouses. Some Muslim clerics voiced concerns about these new social spaces, arguing that they could lead to moral corruption among the faithful.

They believed that coffeehouses, with their stimulating atmosphere and potential for distraction, could intoxicate the minds of the faithful, diverting them from religious duties and righteous behavior.

Despite these concerns, coffeehouses continued to flourish and spread throughout the Ottoman Empire and beyond.

By the 17th century, coffeehouses had become popular across Europe, from London to Vienna, Paris to Amsterdam.

Each city developed its own unique coffeehouse culture, reflecting local tastes, customs, and social norms.

The legacy of these early coffeehouses persists today in the modern café culture that spans the globe. They remain symbols of community, intellectual exchange, and the universal love for coffee.

ESPRESSO ESPIONAGE: STARBUCKS AT THE CIA!

Nestled within the heart of the CIA headquarters in Langley, Virginia, lies a coffee shop so clandestine that it could rival any espionage operation.

This isn't your average Starbucks; it's a highly secure establishment reserved exclusively for CIA employees and personnel.

Forget casual coffee runs. Access to this covert coffee shop is strictly controlled, and even the act of getting coffee becomes a carefully orchestrated affair.

CIA staff are escorted to and from their posts with the precision and secrecy befitting top-secret agents, ensuring that operations remain discreet and secure.

But what about the baristas? They're not your ordinary coffee makers either.

To earn a role as a barista at the CIA's Starbucks, candidates must undergo a rigorous screening process that rivals the scrutiny of an action movie audition.

What sets this CIA Starbucks apart isn't just its secrecy; it's the unique blend of security and camaraderie that defines the agency's culture.

Amidst the high-stakes world of intelligence gathering, this hidden coffee oasis serves as a rare sanctuary where agents can unwind, recharge, and connect over a cup of coffee - all while safeguarding national security secrets.

The existence of the CIA's Starbucks adds a fascinating layer to the agency's mystique, showcasing their commitment to operational security and the importance of maintaining a sense of normalcy even in the most covert of environments.

GET FROTHY FOR CAFÉ-STYLE COFFEE AT HOME!

Tip #6

Creating the perfect frothy milk for your coffee at home can elevate your beverage to cafe-quality standards. Here's a helpful tip to achieve that:

Start by using cold milk, preferably whole milk for the creamiest froth.

Pour the desired amount into a metal pitcher or a microwave-safe glass jar with a lid. Heat the milk until it is warm, but not boiling—around 150-160°F (65-70°C) is ideal.

Next, immerse a milk frother into the milk and froth it until it reaches your desired consistency, holding the frother slightly off-center to encourage the frothing process.

COFFEE MAKES EVERYTHING BETTER

COFFEE ON THE GO: THE CAR-PUCCINO ADVENTURE!

In a remarkable display of ingenuity and innovation, the year 2010 witnessed a stunning transformation in the automotive world.

A 1988 Volkswagen Scirocco, a classic car beloved for its sleek design and performance, underwent a magical twist — it was ingeniously modified to run on leftover coffee grounds!

This caffeinated wonder made headlines when it was featured on the popular TV show 'Bang Goes the Theory'.

The concept was as bold as it was unconventional: using coffee grounds, a byproduct of the beloved beverage, to power a vehicle.

Despite initial skepticism, the coffee-fueled car not only moved but exceeded expectations by zooming an astonishing 209 miles on a single charge of coffee grounds.

To put this into perspective, that's roughly equivalent to traveling one mile for every 56 espressos brewed!

But the surprises didn't end there. This java juggernaut didn't just putter along; it reached speeds of up to 60 miles per hour, proving that coffee isn't just for sipping but also for cruising in style.

The coffee-powered Volkswagen Scirocco serves as a testament to human creativity and the potential for sustainable energy solutions.

By harnessing the energy locked within coffee grounds, a common waste product, innovators demonstrated the feasibility of alternative fuel sources while capturing imaginations worldwide.

DECAF DILEMMA: SIP OR SPLIT!

In the vibrant and culturally rich Ottoman Empire of the 16th century, coffee played a surprising role in marital dynamics.

A unique tradition emerged where the provision of coffee by a husband to his family became not just a gesture of hospitality but a critical aspect of marital harmony.

If a husband failed to supply enough coffee for his household, his wife had the grounds — quite literally — to seek divorce.

This caffeinated twist on marital bliss underscored the cultural significance and daily importance of coffee in Ottoman society.

As the empire transitioned into the following century, a dramatic shift occurred. Authorities initiated a harsh crackdown on coffee consumption, culminating in an outright ban on the beloved beverage.

This wasn't merely a matter of prohibiting a popular drink; the coffee ban came with severe consequences.

Those caught savoring the forbidden brew faced punishments that ranged from public floggings and severe beatings to, in extreme cases, death.

The stringent enforcement of the coffee ban marked a significant cultural and legal shift, reflecting broader social and political changes within the Ottoman Empire during that era.

The rollercoaster ride of coffee's history in the Ottoman Empire - from being a catalyst for marital discord to facing a ruthless prohibition - highlights the complex interplay between culture, tradition, and authority.

It serves as a poignant reminder of the profound impact that seemingly innocuous beverages have had on societal norms and individual freedoms throughout history.

DOUBLE-DIP YOUR BREW!

Tip #7

Keeping your coffee grounds can be surprisingly beneficial in various ways.

Firstly, used coffee grounds make excellent natural fertilizers for plants due to their high nitrogen content, which helps to promote healthy growth and enhance soil structure.

Additionally, coffee grounds can be repurposed as an effective abrasive cleaner for scrubbing surfaces like sinks and countertops, thanks to their texture and natural acidity.

They also serve as a natural odor absorber, whether placed in the refrigerator to neutralize food smells or used as a deodorizer in shoes.

Moreover, coffee grounds can be used in DIY beauty treatments, such as exfoliating scrubs and masks, offering skin benefits through their antioxidant properties.

OCD
OBSESSIVE COFFEE DRINKER

SIPHON METHOD

EQUIPMENT NEEDED:
· Siphon coffee maker · Freshly ground coffee beans ·
Kettle · Timer · Stirring utensil · Mug or carafe

STEP 1
Preheat water in a kettle to just below boiling, around 200°F (93°C).

STEP 2
Pour the hot water into the lower chamber. Use the desired amount of water based on the number of servings you want.

STEP 3
Place the lower chamber with water on the siphon stand and light the burner beneath it. The heat will cause the water to move up into the upper chamber.

STEP 4
Use about 30 grams of coffee for 500 grams of water. Grind the coffee to a medium consistency, similar to table salt.

STEP 5
Once the water has moved into the upper chamber and is just below boiling, add the ground coffee. Stir gently to ensure all grounds are saturated.

STEP 6
Start your timer and let the coffee brew for about 1-1.5 minutes. Stir the coffee gently during this time to promote even extraction. Extinguish the burner. As the lower chamber cools, it creates a vacuum that pulls the brewed coffee down through the filter and into the lower chamber.

STEP 7
Once all the coffee has been drawn down, remove the upper chamber. Stir the coffee in the lower chamber to mix the flavors evenly. Pour the coffee into your mug or carafe and enjoy.

THE BEST CUPS

Tip #8

Choosing the right cup for your coffee can significantly enhance your drinking experience.

Opting for porcelain or glass cups is ideal because they are non-porous, which prevents any oils or flavors from being absorbed into the cup.

This ensures that each sip maintains the pure taste of your coffee without any unwanted residues.

Ceramic cups, while also popular, can sometimes have rougher surfaces or natural glazes that may subtly alter the coffee's flavor profile, which may not always be desirable.

Ultimately, selecting a cup that preserves the integrity of your coffee's flavor while aligning with your personal preferences for texture and style can make a noticeable difference in how enjoyable each cup of coffee tastes.

COSMIC CAFFEINE

Believe it or not, astronauts were enjoying coffee even before they set foot on the Moon in 1969.

In the early days, however, enjoying coffee in space posed significant challenges. Without the luxury of gravity, handling liquid beverages like coffee could lead to messy mishaps.

Fast forward to the present day, and advancements in space technology have revolutionized how astronauts enjoy their coffee beyond Earth's atmosphere.

Enter vacuum-sealed pouches designed to contain liquids in zero gravity, anti-gravity cups that prevent spills, and specially engineered space-safe coffee machines.

These innovations have banished the spillage dramas that once plagued astronauts in the final frontier, ensuring that coffee breaks in space are as smooth and enjoyable as possible.

Coffee in space isn't just a dream; it's a celestial reality that reflects humanity's ingenuity and desire for comfort even amidst the vastness of space.

After all, why should Earth have all the fun when there's a whole universe waiting to be caffeinated?

From early missions to modern space expeditions, coffee remains a symbol of familiarity and comfort, bridging the gap between the extraordinary challenges of space exploration and the everyday pleasures of home.

STIR IT UP!

Tip #9

Enhancing your coffee with flavors like cinnamon, nutmeg, and other spices can elevate your brew to new heights of taste and aroma.

Start by selecting fresh, high-quality spices for the best results. Experiment by adding ground spices directly into your coffee grounds before brewing to infuse the flavors seamlessly.

If using whole spices like cinnamon sticks or nutmeg, grind them fresh just before adding to maximize their potency.

Alternatively, flavored syrups and natural extracts offer convenient ways to sweeten and flavor your coffee. Adjust the amount of spice or syrup to suit your taste preferences, keeping in mind that spices can be quite potent. Adding flavors can be a delightful way to customize your brew.

A TIMELESS SIP!

Coffee has a rich history dating back to 800 A.D. According to legend, the discovery of coffee's stimulating effects is attributed to a goat herder in the 9th century.

As the story goes, the herder noticed that his goats became unusually lively and energetic after eating the red berries from a certain tree.

Intrigued by this behavior, he decided to try the berries himself and experienced a similar surge of energy.

This serendipitous discovery eventually led to the cultivation and spread of coffee as a beloved beverage around the world.

Today, coffee remains a staple in many cultures, cherished for its invigorating properties and rich flavors derived from the roasted seeds of the coffee plant.

BRAZIL, THE JAVA JUGGERNAUT!

Brazil isn't just a country — it's a powerhouse in the world of coffee production!

Proudly supplying more than one-third of the world's coffee, Brazil stands as a towering figure in the global coffee industry, surpassing even the formidable output of countries like Vietnam.

What's their secret sauce? It's a combination of factors that contribute to Brazil's coffee dominance.

First and foremost are the unparalleled natural advantages found in Brazil's diverse landscapes and climates.

From the rolling hills of Minas Gerais to the sprawling plantations of São Paulo and Bahia, Brazil offers ideal conditions for cultivating coffee.

The rich soil, ample rainfall, and varying altitudes create microclimates that are perfect for growing different coffee varietals, each with its own unique flavor profile.

But it's not just about quantity; it's about the quality and craftsmanship that Brazilian coffee producers bring to each bean.

Brazilian coffee farmers have honed their skills over generations, mastering cultivation techniques that ensure consistency and excellence in every harvest.

From meticulous harvesting and processing methods to rigorous quality control measures, Brazilian coffee embodies a dedication to excellence that has made it synonymous with premium coffee worldwide.

For coffee lovers, Brazil is more than just a provider of beans; it's a paradise where every cup tells a story of passion and tradition.

CHEMEX METHOD

EQUIPMENT NEEDED:
· Chemex coffee maker · Chemex paper filter · Kettle ·
Timer · Stirring utensil · Freshly ground coffee beans

STEP 1
Heat water to about 200°F (93°C). If you don't have a thermometer, bring the water to a boil and let it sit for about 30 seconds.

STEP 2
Fold the Chemex paper filter and place it into the Chemex with the triple-layered side facing the spout. Rinse the filter with hot water to remove any paper taste and to preheat the Chemex.

STEP 3
For a standard 6-cup Chemex, use about 30 grams of coffee and 450 grams of water. Grind the coffee to a medium-coarse consistency, similar to sea salt.

STEP 4
Add the ground coffee to the filter. Gently shake to level the grounds. Start your timer and pour just enough hot water to saturate the grounds evenly. This is called the "bloom" and allows the coffee to degas. Let it sit for about 30-45 seconds.

STEP 5
After the bloom, begin pouring water slowly in a circular motion, starting from the center and moving outward, then back to the center. Continue pouring in stages, maintain a consistent water level in the filter. Aim to complete the pour within 3-4 minutes.

STEP 6
Once you have poured the desired amount of water, let the coffee continue to drip through the filter into the Chemex. The total brewing time should be around 4-5 minutes. Once the dripping has stopped, remove the filter. Give the Chemex a gentle swirl to mix the coffee and serve immediately.

MY BIRTHSTONE IS A COFFEE BEAN

THE WORLD'S PRICIEST BREW!

Kopi Luwak stands out as one of the most expensive and exotic coffees globally, renowned for its distinctive production process.

The coffee beans used in Kopi Luwak undergo a truly unconventional journey before reaching your cup.

Native to Indonesia, this coffee is produced from beans that have been partially digested by the Indonesian Palm Civet, a small mammal known for its selective feeding habits.

In the wild, civets consume ripe coffee cherries, digesting the fleshy pulp while the coffee beans inside remain intact.

During digestion, enzymes in the civet's stomach alter the chemical composition of the beans, breaking down proteins and imparting unique flavors.

The beans are then excreted in the animal's feces, where they are carefully collected by farmers. Once collected, the Kopi Luwak beans undergo a meticulous cleaning process.

They are washed thoroughly to remove any remaining traces of the civet's digestive enzymes and fecal matter.

This cleaning process is often done by hand, ensuring that only the highest quality beans are selected for further processing.

After washing, the beans are typically dried and then roasted to bring out their unique flavors.

The roasting process is crucial in developing Kopi Luwak's distinctive profile, which is often described as smooth and complex, with reduced acidity due to the enzymes breaking down during digestion.

The washing process, which involves filtering the beans through volcanic rock beds, further refines their flavor profile by removing excess oils and acids.

When brewed using high-quality spring water, Kopi Luwak delivers a uniquely smooth and rich coffee experience that captivates connoisseurs around the world.

TYPES OF COFFEE

Espresso	Doppio	Lungo
ESPRESSO	2x ESPRESSO	WATER / ESPRESSO

Flat White	Macchiato	Latte Macchiato
STEAMED MILK / ESPRESSO	TOP OF FOAMED MILK / ESPRESSO	FOAMED MILK / ESPRESSO / STEAMED MILK

Irish	Con Panna	Cocoa
WHIPPED CREAM / WHISKY / ESPRESSO	WHIPPED CREAM / ESPRESSO	MILK / COCOA

TYPES OF COFFEE

Americano	Cappuccino	Latte
WATER / ESPRESSO	FOAMED MILK / STEAMED MILK / ESPRESSO	FOAMED MILK / STEAMED MILK / ESPRESSO

Ristretto	Mocha	White Mocha
CONCENTRATED ESPRESSO	FOAMED MILK / STEAMED MILK / CHOCOLATE / ESPRESSO	FOAMED MILK / STEAMED MILK / WHITE CHOCOLATE / ESPRESSO

Marrochino	Vienna	Breve
FOAMED MILK / COCOA / ESPRESSO	WHIPPED CREAM & COCOA POWDER / ESPRESSO	FOAMED MILK / HALF-AND-HALF MILK / ESPRESSO

SIP FOR LIFE!

Recent research suggests that consuming three to four cups of coffee daily may contribute to a longer and healthier lifespan.

This finding has sparked interest and curiosity among coffee enthusiasts and health-conscious individuals alike.

Moderate coffee consumption has been linked to a range of health benefits, supported by numerous studies.

These benefits include a reduced risk of developing several chronic conditions that can affect lifespan and quality of life.

Among the notable conditions are Parkinson's disease, cardiovascular disease, Alzheimer's disease, and depression.

The secret behind these potential health benefits lies in the chemical composition of coffee beans.

Two key compounds, chlorogenic acid and caffeic acid, play significant roles. These compounds are powerful antioxidants that help neutralize harmful free radicals in the body.

Free radicals are unstable molecules that can damage cells and contribute to the development of various diseases.

By increasing the body's levels of antioxidants, chlorogenic and caffeic acids found in coffee contribute to overall health and well-being.

Antioxidants help protect cells from oxidative stress, inflammation, and other processes that can lead to chronic diseases over time.

It's important to note that while moderate coffee consumption may offer health benefits, excessive intake should be avoided, as it can lead to negative side effects such as insomnia, jitteriness, and increased heart rate in sensitive individuals.

The optimal amount of coffee varies among individuals and can depend on factors such as tolerance to caffeine and overall health status.

BUY A BURR!

Tip #10

Grinding coffee beans might seem simple, but achieving consistency is key to a perfect brew.

Uneven grounds can lead to unpredictable extraction, affecting the balance and flavor of your coffee.

Enter the burr grinder: a coffee enthusiast's best friend. Unlike blade grinders, burr grinders crush beans into uniform particles, ensuring each piece is the ideal size for optimal extraction.

This precision results in a balanced, flavorful cup every time. Embrace the burr grinder as your conductor for extracting the full symphony of flavors from your favorite beans, elevating your coffee experience to new heights of perfection.

COFFEE'S FLAVORFUL SYMPHONY

Coffee boasts over six times the number of distinct aromas compared to wine.

With approximately 1,500 different aromatic differences discernible in coffee, compared to around 200 tasting notes found in wine, coffee connoisseurs have a broad palette to explore.

Both professional wine and coffee tasters employ similar methods to evaluate and describe these beverages.

They meticulously assess factors such as aromas, flavors, textures, body, and acidity to discern the nuances and quality of each cup or glass, respectively.

This shared approach highlights the artistry and precision involved in tasting and appreciating these beloved beverages.

THE ULTIMATE LOW-CAL SUPERHERO!

Behold the simplicity of black coffee, a beverage revered for its minimalism with a mere one calorie per cup.

It stands as the undisputed low-calorie superhero of the coffee world — a guilt-free sip that feels like a victory lap in the quest for health-conscious choices.

Once you venture beyond black coffee into the realm of milk, syrups, and sweeteners, you've embarked on a calorie rollercoaster ride.

Adding just a splash of whole milk or a drizzle of flavored syrup can significantly increase the caloric content of your cup.

Consider the more extravagant offerings from popular coffee chains like Starbucks, where a seemingly innocent coffee break can morph into a full-blown culinary adventure.

Some specialty creations, laden with whipped cream, caramel drizzles, and indulgent toppings, can pack a whopping 600 calories or more.

It's a gentle reminder that even in the seemingly innocuous world of coffee, calories can sneak in when you least expect them.

Whether you prefer a simple black coffee for its minimal calorie impact or indulge in elaborate coffee creations as a treat, being mindful of your coffee choices can contribute to a balanced diet and lifestyle.

PERCOLATOR

EQUIPMENT NEEDED:
· Percolator (stovetop) · Freshly ground coffee beans ·
Water · Heat source · Coffee measuring scoop

STEP 1
Remove the lid, coffee grounds basket, and stem from the percolator. Fill the percolator's bottom chamber with cold water.

STEP 2
A common ratio is one tablespoon of coffee per cup of water. Use a medium-coarse grind, similar to the texture of coarse sea salt.

STEP 3
Place the stem into the bottom chamber. Fill the coffee grounds basket with the measured coffee and place it on the stem. Ensure the lid is securely attached to the basket to prevent grounds from falling into the water. Place the lid on the percolator.

STEP 4
Place the percolator on a medium heat source on your stovetop. Monitor the heat to ensure the water does not boil too vigorously.

STEP 5
As the water heats, it will rise through the stem and spread over the coffee grounds, then drip back down into the water chamber. This cycle will repeat. The typical brewing time is about 7-10 minutes, depending on your desired strength.

STEP 6
Adjust the heat as necessary to maintain a steady perking rate, where you see a regular but gentle cycle of bubbles. Too rapid a boil can lead to over-extraction and bitterness.

STEP 7
Carefully remove the lid, coffee grounds basket, and stem to prevent any grounds from falling into the coffee. Pour the brewed coffee into your mug.

BERRY BREW!

Did you know that despite its name, the coffee "bean" isn't truly a bean at all? Rather, it is the pit or seed found inside a vibrant red fruit known as the coffee cherry.

This cherry-like fruit grows on coffee trees, and it takes approximately eight months for the cherries to ripen fully before they are harvested.

Interestingly, the sweet pulp of the coffee cherry is considered a delicacy among several wild animals, showcasing a unique ecological relationship in coffee-growing regions.

Animals such as elephants, bats, and monkeys are known to enjoy the fruity pulp, often consuming the cherries and subsequently spreading the coffee seeds through their droppings.

This process not only aids in the dispersal of coffee plants but also contributes to the biodiversity of coffee ecosystems.

Wake Up and Smell the Coffee

COFFEE WORLD CHAMPION!

Salesman Albert Baker set a very delicious world record!

Albert Baker was an avid coffee lover, and in 1926, he drank a massive 157 eight-ounce cups of coffee in 6 hours and 20 minutes, breaking the world record.

By 1928, he was a known legend, and broke his own record after making an appearance in Los Angeles, by drinking 280 cups of coffee in just 4 and a half hours!

His crusade carried on, as he challenged any willing competitor into a coffee-drinking competition, and defeated 115 opponents (the nearest drinking only 150 cups in 4 hours).

COFFEE RULES THE SIP!

Coffee holds an unparalleled place as the world's most beloved beverage, with an astonishing 2 billion cups enjoyed each day, and an astronomical 400 billion cups consumed annually across the globe.

Finland emerges as the undisputed champion in per capita coffee consumption. With an average of over 12 kilograms (26 pounds) of coffee consumed per person annually, Finns have elevated coffee to a cultural cornerstone.

In Finland, coffee isn't merely a beverage but a cherished tradition woven into the fabric of daily life. This dedication is reflected in Finnish work culture, where employees are legally entitled to not one, but two ten-minute coffee breaks during their workday.

These breaks serve as cherished moments of relaxation and socialization, fostering camaraderie and productivity in the workplace.

Beyond the workplace, coffee in Finland is a social ritual, enjoyed with friends and family in homes, cafés, and even outdoor settings year-round.

The love for coffee runs deep, with Finns taking pride in their coffee brewing techniques and preferences, whether it's enjoying a strong black brew or indulging in specialty coffee preparations.

In essence, coffee in Finland transcends mere refreshment—it's a way of life, intricately tied to the country's culture, traditions, and social interactions.

Amidst the Northern Lights and endless landscapes, coffee remains a constant source of joy and comfort, symbolizing warmth, hospitality, and community in the heart of every Finnish coffee enthusiast.

COFFEE ISN'T JUST A DRINK

BLACK COFFEE:
Simple and straightforward, black coffee lovers tend to be quiet, moody, and mysterious!

ESPRESSO:
Like the drink, espresso lovers share a bold and intense personality, and tend to be well-traveled.

CAPPUCCINO:
Sensitive yet adventurous, Cappuccino lovers share a love for perfection!

FLAVORED COFFEE:
Creative and imaginative, flavored coffee drinkers can often be impulsive or stressed.

DECAF:
Cautious and observant, decaf drinkers can be obsessive over their coffee drinking.

LATTE:
Latte drinkers are often seen as flirty and outgoing, with a love for class and style.

KEEP IT FRESH!

Tip #11

Invest in freshly roasted coffee beans and grind them just before brewing. Coffee beans start losing their freshness and flavor shortly after roasting.

To ensure the best-tasting coffee, purchase whole beans from a reputable roaster and grind them right before brewing.

This preserves the beans' aromatic oils and flavors, resulting in a richer and more flavorful cup of coffee.

Adjust the grind size based on your brewing method—coarser for French press and finer for espresso machines—to achieve optimal extraction and taste.

KING CHARLES II'S COFFEE SHOP CRACKDOWN!

In 1675, during the reign of King Charles II of England, a surprising edict was issued that shook the burgeoning coffee culture of London: a ban on coffee shops.

King Charles II, suspicious of these establishments, believed they were becoming hotbeds of political dissent and conspiracy against his rule.

He argued that coffeehouses fostered "very evil and dangerous effects" and disrupted public peace and order.

The decree sent shockwaves through English society, where coffeehouses had become popular hubs for intellectual discourse, socializing, and business transactions.

These establishments were frequented by writers, merchants, politicians, and scholars who engaged in lively debates and exchanged ideas over cups of coffee.

The ban threatened to stifle these intellectual exchanges and social interactions that had become integral to London's cultural and commercial life.

However, the ban on coffee shops sparked widespread outrage among English citizens.

Recognizing the public outcry and the economic importance of coffeehouses, the ban was eventually lifted, and coffee shops resumed their operations shortly after.

The decision to revoke the ban underscored the resilience of coffee culture and the significant role that coffeehouses played in the social and intellectual fabric of London.

Following the reinstatement of coffee shops, these establishments continued to thrive as centers of enlightenment and cultural exchange throughout the 18th and 19th centuries.

BEYOND THE NEED FOR SPEED!

The term 'Espresso' is often misunderstood as meaning 'fast coffee,' but its true origin lies in the method of preparation.

Derived from the Italian word 'esprimere,' which translates to 'to press out' or 'to express,' Espresso refers to the process of tightly packing finely ground coffee into a portafilter and then forcing hot water through the grounds under high pressure.

This method extracts a concentrated shot of coffee with a rich, velvety crema on top — a hallmark of a well-made espresso.

Italians have a deep-rooted passion for coffee, considering it an essential part of their daily routine and culture.

Coffee consumption in Italy isn't just about caffeine; it's a social ritual that spans generations and binds communities together.

Whether enjoyed solo at a bustling espresso bar or shared among friends at a leisurely café, coffee plays a central role in Italian social life.

Reflecting this reverence for coffee, the Italian government has established regulations to uphold the standards of espresso preparation.

These regulations dictate everything from the quality of the coffee beans used to the precise brewing parameters, ensuring consistency and excellence in every cup.

This commitment to quality underscores Italy's dedication to preserving the art and tradition of espresso-making - a craft that has transcended borders to become a global symbol of Italian culinary heritage.

STRESSED BLESSED AND COFFEE obsessed

KEEP YOUR COFFEE CLEAN!

Tip #11

Despite regular machine cleanings, sneaky residue can hide in hard-to-reach places.

Coffee oils are the culprit, gradually building up and dulling the flavor of your brew.

To combat this, use cotton swabs to meticulously clean those elusive spots where residue accumulates.

Make it a daily ritual to maintain your coffee machine's freshness and ensure every cup shines with rich, flavorful coffee.

COFFEE'S FLAVOR ODYSSEY!

Similar to fine wine, coffee embodies a concept known as 'coffee terroir,' where the flavors of the beans reflect the unique characteristics of their growing regions.

Just as wine connoisseurs appreciate how grapes express their terroir through aroma and taste, coffee enthusiasts delight in the diverse flavors and profiles shaped by coffee-growing regions worldwide.

Coffee terroir encompasses a range of factors that influence the beans' flavor, aroma, and quality.

Soil composition, climate variations, altitude, and specific microclimates all play pivotal roles in shaping the personality of coffee beans.

For instance, beans grown in volcanic soil may exhibit notes of earthiness and minerality, while those cultivated in high-altitude regions might showcase bright acidity and floral aromas.

Furthermore, the processing methods employed after harvesting — whether wet-processed, dry-processed, or semi-washed — further contribute to the final flavor profile of the coffee.

These methods influence how the beans retain moisture, ferment, and develop their distinctive flavors during drying and milling.

The result is a delightful tapestry of coffee flavors that captivate the palate with their complexity and nuance.

From the fruity and vibrant coffees of Ethiopia's Yirgacheffe region to the chocolatey richness of beans from Colombia's Andean slopes, each origin tells a story through its beans, inviting coffee lovers on a sensory journey around the globe.

THE BIRTH OF COFFEE CULTURE!

Coffeehouses, renowned as the original "Penny Universities," offered more than just a caffeine fix - they provided a gateway to intellectual enlightenment and lively discourse.

In the early days, for the price of a single cup of coffee, patrons gained access to a vibrant hub where ideas flowed as freely as the coffee itself.

These establishments were not mere cafés; they were epicenters of intellectual exchange and debate.

Patrons engaged in spirited conversations that rivaled the intellectual rigor of traditional universities.

Discussions spanned politics, philosophy, literature, science, and beyond, attracting a diverse crowd of thinkers, writers, artists, and revolutionaries.

Coffeehouses became synonymous with enlightenment and innovation, where minds percolated with new ideas and perspectives.

They fostered an atmosphere that encouraged creativity and critical thinking, challenging conventional wisdom and sparking intellectual revolutions.

It was in these bustling coffeehouses that new concepts were born, friendships flourished, and alliances were forged.

The emergence of coffee as the favored beverage of these "Penny Universities" symbolized a cultural shift towards inclusivity and accessibility.

Unlike exclusive academic institutions, coffeehouses welcomed individuals from all walks of life, transcending social barriers and fostering a sense of community among patrons.

THE PRICE OF BEANS

Coffee's global influence extends far beyond its role as a beloved morning ritual—it stands as one of the most traded commodities worldwide, second only to oil.

This remarkable status underscores coffee's profound impact on global economies, particularly in regions across Central and South America, Africa, and Asia.

The cultivation and trade of coffee beans are integral to the economies of numerous countries, providing livelihoods for millions of farmers, exporters, and laborers.

From the misty highlands of Ethiopia to the sprawling coffee plantations of Brazil, coffee production supports communities, drives economic growth, and shapes cultural identities.

The global coffee market is a dynamic landscape where beans are traded on commodity exchanges and through direct trade relationships.

Coffee beans pass through a complex supply chain — from farms to processing facilities, exporters, roasters, and finally to consumers worldwide.

This intricate network connects people and nations, fostering economic ties and cultural exchange over a shared love for the brew.

Moreover, coffee's popularity transcends borders and cultures, uniting people from diverse backgrounds in their appreciation for its rich flavors and stimulating properties.

Whether enjoyed in bustling cafes in Paris, sidewalk stalls in Addis Ababa, or specialty shops in Tokyo, coffee serves as a universal language that bridges gaps and sparks conversations.

In conclusion, coffee's status as one of the world's most traded commodities highlights its pivotal role in global trade and commerce.

COFFEE IN COCKTAILS:
ICED WHISKEY COFFEE

Add cold coffee, whiskey syrup, and whiskey to a glass over ice, then stir well. Top with whipped cream and sprinkle with cinnamon.

MEXICAN COFFEE

Combine Kahlúa and tequila, then add hot coffee and stir gently. Add whipped cream, cinnamon and a cinnamon stick for an added treat!

ESPRESSO NEGRONI

Add gin, sweet vermouth and Campari into a glass over ice, add an orange twist, then pour cold espresso over a spoon on top.

ESPRESSO MARTINI

Add chilled espresso, ice, vodka, Baileys, Kahlúa, syrup, and whole milk into a shaker, and shake for 20 seconds, then pour and serve!

COLD BREW BOURBON COCKTAIL

Make cold brew coffee, add bourbon, maple syrup, and cream. Add a dash of triple sec, then stir and serve!

LONG ISLAND ICED COFFEE

Shake together coffee, Baileys, Kahlúa, vodka, rum, and tequila – and serve over ice!

DON'T USE BUDGET BEANS!

Tip #12

Exploring the realm of coffee beans can feel like unraveling a secret code. Opting for cheaper beans might compromise freshness, affecting the flavor profile you crave.

The secret lies not only in seeking freshness but also in selecting beans that match your taste preferences.

If you prefer a lighter coffee with a more delicate taste, aim for light or medium roasts. These roasts preserve more of the beans' natural characteristics, offering nuanced flavors and brighter acidity.

On the other hand, if you crave a bolder, more intense experience, venture into the realm of dark roasts. Dark roasts boast robust flavors, with caramelized sugars and deeper, smokier notes that satisfy those who prefer a richer coffee profile.

FIRST I DRINK THE coffee THEN I DO THE THINGS

WHICH COFFEE, WHICH MUG?

CLASSIC:
A ceramic or porcelain cup – works perfectly for all types of coffee.

ESPRESSO:
Small, holds the perfect amount for espresso.

CAPPUCCINO:
Wide and shallow, usually made from ceramic or porcelain.

LATTE:
Tall and narrow, allows layers to sit well.

LATTE MACCHIATO GLASS:
Non-porous clear glass, shows the layers of milk, espresso, and foam.

GIBRALTAR GLASS:
A thick glass cup, perfect for cortado or flat white.

BOWL:
Large and round, typically used for cafe au lait.

IRISH COFFEE GLASS:
Glass cup with a handle that holds 8 to 10 ounces of Irish coffee.

FRESH? DO THE TEST!

Tip #13

Curious about the freshness of your coffee beans? Here's a straightforward method to gauge it: Take a handful of beans, place them in a ziplock bag, squeeze out the excess air, and seal it. Leave the bag overnight.

The next morning, check the bag. If it's puffed up like a pillow, congratulations! Your beans are fresh and ready to brew. This indicates that they are still releasing carbon dioxide, a sign of freshness.

On the other hand, if the bag remains flat like a pancake, it suggests that your beans have lost some freshness. This can affect the flavor and quality of your coffee. Freshness is crucial for a delicious brew that's always at its peak.

DITCH THE DEHYDRATION!

Coffee often gets a bad rap for being dehydrating, but contrary to popular belief, it's not as detrimental to hydration as once thought.

Yes, coffee is a natural diuretic, which means it can increase urine production and make your bladder work a bit harder. However, the diuretic effect of coffee is relatively mild compared to other beverages like alcohol.

Moreover, the water content in a cup of coffee is sufficient to offset its diuretic effect. In fact, studies have shown that moderate coffee consumption doesn't lead to significant dehydration.

This means that enjoying your favorite cup of coffee, even on a hot summer day, won't leave you severely dehydrated.

CELEBRITIES WHO LOVE THEIR COFFEE:

HUGH JACKMAN:

Wolverine loves coffee? Yes! On a visit to Kochere, Ethiopia, Jackman met a joyful coffee farmer named Dukale. Moved by his story, Jackman vowed to improve the lives of coffee farmers, and founded Laughing Man Coffee, providing farmers with education and resources.

RALPH LAUREN:

When he's not creating the next biggest fashion statement, Lauren can be found enjoying a coffee in his Manhattan coffee shop, Ralph's Coffee. During the global pandemic in 2020, Lauren delivered coffee and baked treats to front-line workers around New York for free, to show his gratitude for their hard work – what a champ!

MARTHA STEWART:

Known for her cookbooks and talk shows, Stewart used her foodie knowledge and partnered with a nutritionist, to create ULIVjava, coffee that's organic, fair-trade, and filled to the rim with minerals and vitamins – who thought coffee could be any healthier?

ROB ZOMBIE:

Despite his scary exterior, this horror movie legend really cares about quality and sustainability. He collaborated with Dead Sled Coffee, to make his 'Hellbilly Brew' - made from 100% Arabica beans, and the company's first 100% certified USDA organic coffee.
What a legend!

FANCY A CUP OF JOE?

The expression 'a cup of joe' is a colloquial term widely used to refer to coffee, but its exact origin remains a subject of debate and folklore. One popular theory traces its beginnings to 1914 in the United States Navy.

Legend has it that the phrase emerged after the Navy's Secretary, Josephus Daniels, banned alcohol on all Navy ships.

With sailors deprived of their beloved rum ration, coffee became the beverage of choice, earning it the nickname 'cup of joe' in honor of Secretary Daniels.

NO PRESSURE!

Tip #14

Mastering a few crucial steps for French press aficionados is the key.

Once you've allowed the coffee grounds to settle at the bottom of the pot, exercise patience for a few minutes before gently pressing down the plunger.

This crucial step allows the flavors to fully infuse, resulting in a more robust and satisfying cup of coffee.

When using the plunger, avoid pressing all the way down to the bottom. Leave a slight gap to prevent sediment from escaping, ensuring a clean and pristine pour into your cup. This small yet significant detail enhances your French press experience, transforming it from good to exceptional.

A LIFETIME SUPPLY OF HAPPINESS!

Starbucks, a global powerhouse in the coffee industry, stands as a beacon for coffee lovers worldwide with its commitment to delivering delicious java experiences.

With a massive customer base and a penchant for quality, it's no surprise that a enormous amount of resources are required to meet demand.

To keep pace with their coffee production, Starbucks procures and uses an astounding 93 million gallons of milk each year.

To put this into perspective, that volume could fill approximately 155 Olympic-sized swimming pools.

In addition to milk, Starbucks goes through a substantial number of paper cups annually — approximately 2.3 billion.

DRINK YOUR coffee

IT'S CHAOS OUT THERE

TOP NOTCH COFFEE

Tip #15

Are you looking to enhance the taste of your coffee? Troubleshoot most issues with just a few simple adjustments!

If your coffee is too weak: Use less water and increase the amount of coffee grounds. Grinding your coffee beans finer can also help extract more flavor.

If your coffee is too strong: Use more water and decrease the amount of coffee grounds.

If your coffee tastes too bitter: Try using a coarser grind and shorten the blooming time. This can reduce over-extraction, which causes bitterness.

If your coffee tastes too sour: Use a finer grind and lengthen the blooming time. This allows for more extraction of flavors without the acidity overpowering the brew.

THIS COFFEE IS UNPRECEDENTED!

Did you know, US coffee brand Maxwell House has a famous president to thank for their timeless slogan?

26th US President Teddy Roosevelt was well known for his love of a beany brew, which started when he was a young boy.

Suffering from Asthma 98 years before inhalers were invented, the doctor's cure was to drink coffee!

In 1907, Roosevelt visited The Hermitage Association, a museum that's located in 7th President Andrew Jackson's former home.

While enjoying a cup of Maxwell House coffee, he was documented to have exclaimed that the coffee was "good to the last drop"!

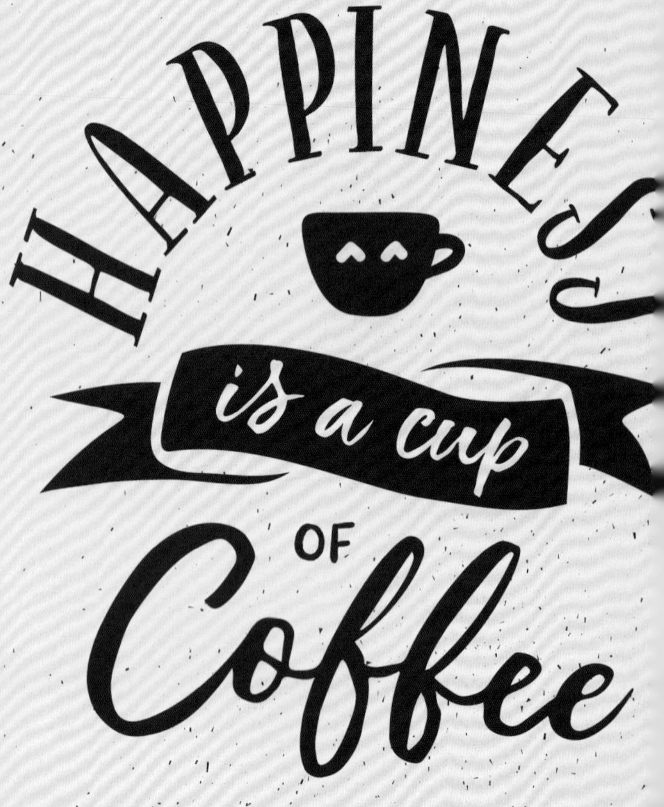
HAPPINES
is a cup
OF
Coffee